From a Builder to a Healer:

THE DAWN OF MY NEW TRUTHS

John L. Povey

ACKNOWLEDGMENTS

I would like to show my appreciation to all the following people who have, in one way or another, been or had a great influence on me and assisted me on my journey up until this point in time.

My wife Lesley, who is my true soul mate, my anchor and editor-in-chief of all that I write whether in this book, or on any of my Facebook posts, thank you again my darling for the many ways in which you support me on my journey. Xx.

To Barbara Wingrove, my Reiki teacher, the person responsible for setting my feet firmly upon the pathway that I now follow, one that still leads me into the unknown where I walk with no fear in my heart.

To Sharon Hall, for being an inspiring mentor and friend, and the Minister that performed our wedding rites for Lesley and I back in 2016.

To Darren Turner, who was also a mentor and taught me back in those early days, and someone that I still count as a friend.

To Margaret Smith, a wonderful mentor who both guided me and gave me that space to grow on my pathway. Sadly, Margaret has now transitioned back home to spirit, but I know that you will still look in from time to time to see what Les and I are doing.

To all the many people around the world who have trusted my team and I to help them self-heal, in doing this you have now become a friend rather than a client.

To those who have taught me and shared their knowledge, to those who have given me their energy when I have needed it, and not forgetting all those people around the world that have helped my team and I share our insight and knowledge, in those far-off corners of the world to add our little bit of light to your own so that we can drive back the darkness, I humbly say, thank you and well done.

To my ever-growing spiritual team of guides and inspirers who have seen fit to continue to use me as a vessel for their sharing of knowledge, I have absolute trust in you all as I know that all the words that you write through me are for the best outcomes of mankind.

To Matt Kidd for helping me in getting the finished drafts of this book completed, including assisting with the indexing.

TABLE OF CONTENTS

INTRODUCTION

This is my second book. It covers the work that I have completed since channelling and writing my first book, *From a Builder to a Healer*.

Since writing that first book, I find that more and more information is being passed to me by the universe and my guides. The information can come to me at any time of day or night, but frequently I am awoken in the small hours of the night and told, "go and write." It is then that clarity reigns and, in that silence, I am given knowledge that both inspires and amazes me.

A little about me. As a child I was what you might call a 'school avoider'; I did all that I could to escape either going to school or working while I was in lessons. As a result, I never fully developed any skills in the subjects that I did not like. When I left school at the early age of fourteen, I was probably little better educated than a primary school child. I knew nothing of science, religions, or any maths above fractions. I never attended art, history or geography classes. I was placed in a 'rural science' class; I was sent to the school allotments to help grow vegetables for the school canteen. I was good at sport, however, and I was even picked to play 'hooker' in the school rugby team during my three years at secondary school. Woodwork was my saving grace even though I was not the best at it.

I left school just before my fifteenth birthday on a Friday, and my father put me in a job as a trainee bricklayer the following Monday. I spent most of my teen years and early adult life drifting from job to job, trade to trade. A spell in the army for three years taught me that I was not going to be a killer of men. I felt that I was more of a peacemaker between antagonists, as I somehow found the correct words that would instantly cool a situation and eventually restore calm.

Much later in my life, only ten years ago at the time of writing, I was awoken with an all-consuming desire to heal people. Consequently, both my partner of twenty-plus years and I took reiki level one, and that day my life changed forever. It was like I was suddenly given the password to the whole universe. When I was at school I hated any form of teaching, but I now found myself embarking on numerous courses and workshops in the pursuit of attaining more qualifications in the healing arts of reiki, crystals, higher dimensional healing and sound therapy.

These channels of information transfer were opened, and I found an ability to channel universal energy for use in healing people.

I am now in my sixty ninth year. My guides, who are many and varied, continue to teach me many more advanced healing techniques. I can replicate these on the people that the universe sends to me to heal.

Over the last couple of years, my guides have gently pushed me along the route of sharing the information that they give to me, in workshops at first, then in the writing of my first book.

They tell me each time that when I learn something new, I should record it and save it for putting in one of the books that they inspire me to write.

This one, *The Dawning of my New Truths*, is all about the revelations that my guides have shown me and told me about.

I hope that in publishing this small, informative alternative view of our eternal soul, I may be able to answer some of your questions regarding why we are here, the purpose of the chakra system, the meaning of the etheric light body, and many more questions.

If you do find this book helpful, please leave a review on the author's page indicating how it helped you. If you do not agree with the words and concepts written here, then it is for your own soul to show you the answers that you may be seeking. As for myself, I have an unshakeable faith in what my guides and the universe tell me, and I will continue to follow the path the universe has placed before me.

CHAPTER ONE:
THE SOUL IN ALL ITS GLORY

I have often been asked, "where is a person's soul?" "What does it look like?" "What does it do for us?" "How does it get into us?"

I have been given this information.

The soul is constructed from the same etheric materials as the universe itself, the same materials as the Source or God, Allah, Buddha or any of the other names that this power source is known by.

How many times have different people told you that the soul resides in the brain, the heart, or out in space somewhere with an ethereal connection to it? Or that the soul has two parts: one within you, and one that resides within your one true love, soul mate or twin flame?

Do you believe that it is your soul that is the host of your spirit energy, that part of you that lives on for eternity and is reincarnated time and time again? Is your soul that etheric link back to Source, God, Buddha or Allah?

What if I told you that there is some truth in all these ideas? What if I told you that your soul is made up of millions of fragments, all interconnected to the one great universal soul? If that is the case, then one thing should stand out from those statements, like a lighthouse on a stormy night, with an iridescent beacon of bright shining light, rotating to shine on everything within its range. Please let me explain in the way that my universal guides have shown me.

Your soul is all those things and so much more. It does have a direct connection through to Source, God, and so on. It also has millions of other connections, so many that the human mind cannot yet comprehend it. It is connected to all your past and future lives, in all the dimensions known and unknown. Would you believe me if I said that to some gifted people, your soul is visible? Well, more on that later in the book.

The soul at creation

The universes were created by the fusion of multiple energy systems, which were the building blocks of matter. When planets, solar systems and universes were simultaneously created by this fusion, there was a large residue of energy that was created by the massive explosion of these colliding energies.

This energy was sentient, as were the planets that had been created. The energy was condensed and powerful and contained all the building blocks (or DNA) of the energies that were fused in the creation of matter. However, unlike the planets' energy which was of a low vibrational frequency, this material was extremely high vibrational and unstable in such a large quantity.

These forces, being sentient, and with the combined knowledge of all the other energies, concluded that this newly created energy needed to be fragmented and dispersed, or what had been created would soon become consumed by this new energy.

This fragmentation process was how all souls were created. The soul came into being as a miniature replica of all these once-great energies, containing traces of all of them. As they were created from this cauldron of energy, they were dispersed all over the newly created universes.

Each in turn was then fragmented into well over five million smaller fragments: each as identical as the next, each a duplicate in miniature of those combined great energies. This ensured that no single energy source would ever become too powerful, like the great dark energy that still prowled the cosmos looking for energies to devour.

If it were not for those three separate energies of the light combining their selves in the way that they did to create an equally powerful opposing force, then none of us would be here today to tell this story. Until that point in time, all energies existed in isolation from one another.

But as it was shown to me in a vision, three energies came together: Gold, Blue and Green. As they moved closer to each other in the face of that dark energy mass, wonderful things began to happen. There formed a perfect white circle that joined all of them together. Then the Green energy moved outside of this circle towards the dark mass. As it did so, a triangle of white light appeared connecting all the energies: two within the circle, one outside. As the dark mass touched the Green energy, there was a massive explosion of power. All the energies that the dark had consumed were released and were again free to roam at will.

Planets, stars and all matter were created as a result of this first battle against the dark. A small percentage of every energy around was now in a state of flux within a huge cloud of energy, randomly organised yet disorganised at the same time.

There was so much of this energy that some fragments were left as large masses where the combined information of the previous energies' knowledge was stored. This is what we know of as the 'Akashic records', 'Halls of knowledge', or the 'Etheric library'; it goes by many names. It is where everything that we ever learn is copied over when our short span of eternity in one form or another expires. The soul, however, does not expire, only the combination of nutrients derived from the planet that it resides upon, which have a limited life cycle before they return to their original state.

The soul is a pure sentient energy. It is self-supporting in that it draws upon the surrounding energy that is all around us. The planets, the sun, the moon, and the earth are all sentient too, and can be drawn upon if only the soul remembers how to. The main bulk elements of the soul are fragmented and scattered throughout the universe and all its associated dimensions. Each fragment is connected to every other fragment; there can be many of these fragments residing in the dimension that you now inhabit. We have been taught that if we came face to face with another version of ourselves, then we would create a paradox and chaos would reign. We will cover more on this theory later in the book.

Other dimensional selves

Have you ever had 'déjà vu'? Well, that is often as near as you can normally get to one of your other dimensional selves. Have you experienced that uncanny feeling when you walk around a corner and know the exact scene that will be revealed to you? It is because one of your other dimensional selves that you are connected to has just walked around that corner before you.

There are many factors that can either influence or deny access to these other dimensional selves. Dreams, for instance, are one way of communicating with our other selves. Have you ever had a vivid dream where you see things as if it is you standing there watching things unfold before you? You were probably looking through the eyes of one of your other selves seeing what is going on in their dimension.

It is just another wonder of the soul's fragmentation conundrum that we will eventually learn more about as our connections grow stronger and multiply, and as we become more connected to far distant parts of the universe.

But for now, please understand that your soul was created many aeons ago. There are no new souls being created, as the energy to do so no longer exists. This is just a snapshot of what our soul is and what it can do with us, for us and to us.

Sleeper Cell

One other thing that we need to understand is that as every fragment of the original soul is an absolute duplicate, should anything become attached directly to that soul, it too will be duplicated continuously into every other fragment no matter how many times it has been incarnated.

To the best of my team's knowledge, there was only ever one instance of this occurring. Because the soul was co-created out of the residual flux energies after the big bang, the dark side of these energies created a single parasitic cell that it implanted into every soul that was ever created, and thus went into every fragmentation of that soul.

My team and I call this cell the 'Sleeper Cell'. It has but one purpose: to tip the balance of a soul in the favour of the dark as opposed to the light. It carries within it all known diseases and a host of mutations that we have not even come across yet. It feeds off negative energy in any and all attempts that it makes in trying to dim the light of all souls.

Now, my team's ultimate purpose is to eradicate this cell for all eternity. As there is not the energy to recreate it again, once it is gone it is gone forever; if it is removed from the original soul itself, then it is simultaneously removed from every duplicate of that soul that may or may not be incarnated at that time. So, with each successful removal, we are not just healing a single person, we are doing well over five million possible fragments in one go.

This subject was the basis of my first channelled workshop given to me many years ago, and, as such, a great deal of my current healing practice is directed at finding and removing this nasty parasite. I am sure that there are other healers around the world who do something similar and call it by different terminology, but, in essence, it is this removal of the cell that is allowing others to awaken sooner.

For me, this workshop took me somewhere that, until then, I had never been to: to the original soul of another person right back to the time it was created. The speeds at which these healings work is mind-blowingly fast.

Under normal circumstances, it takes two sessions to complete the removal of the cell. The first session involves clearing the cell within the etheric heart chakra of the client, which will open the doorway to their true soul connection. One month later, after a period of healing has taken place, we then travel down this connection back through aeons to the point where the cell was placed and destroy it.

Once it is destroyed, we use rose quartz energy to fill the void where the cell was so that the dark cannot infiltrate the space. This is because the waves of healing energy radiate outwards from the point of healing; it is like re-writing the history of that soul.

As I said earlier, this was the first workshop that I was given, and at that time I was told that only advanced and experienced healers would be able to understand and complete this work. By this time, I knew that we are all healers within, so I asked for a way to share it with all healers no matter their modality or ability. Consequently, a further two workshops were channelled to me: a beginner course titled 'Introduction to Energy Healing', and an intermediate follow-on called 'Advanced Chakra Healing'.

I was most grateful to the team for these additional workshops, as I now had the ability to teach an absolute novice all about energy healing and to take them on a journey to being a well-developed powerful healer, with the same abilities that my team had given me to destroy the 'Sleeper Cell'.

Since then, my team have further extended my knowledge and given me another higher-level workshop, 'Advanced Universal Healing', where we go beyond the soul and work on past lives and even the future ones too. On completion of this workshop, the student undergoes spiritual changes that will not only provide them with access to all souls but will also allow them to go through their own soul direct to the source energy itself.

CHAPTER TWO:
CHAKRAS AND THE SOUL

Did you know that chakras, those mini energy centres that regulate and record everything that happens to a soul, are made from the same energy matrix as the soul? Most people know of the seven main chakras: Base, Sacral, Solar Plexus, Heart, Throat, Third eye and Crown. But there are many more within the human bio field. As much has already been recorded about these energy centres, I will not go into them in depth in this book. Suffice to say that as a healer, I make full use of both my own chakra system and that of the person being healed.

What I want to pass onto you is that the seven main chakras are also recording devices that record each event within the lifespan of the host body during each incarnation. They store this information until the soul and host separate at death. Then, as the soul rests and reviews what events took place during that incarnation, the stored information is copied over into the Akashic record or Etheric Library.

You may ask why this happens if all the knowledge of the universal energies is already there. The easy answer is that as sentient life evolves, changes take place, both upon the surface of the planet that soul resides upon, and with the interactions between souls on that planet. This interaction between souls is what drives the energy to respond, either the planets' energy or the combined energies of many souls joined in a like-minded cause.

This creates changes in the balance of energies. Being sentient and self-supporting requires a constant flow of energy exchange, and if you disrupt that energy exchange then many things can change within both the human bio field and the planetary bio field.

Earthquakes, tornadoes, tidal waves and volcanoes are all ways through which the earth regulates its energetic balance. The earth has chakras too, and, like a human bio field, if they are unbalanced and in disharmony then illness will run rife throughout the affected areas.

If the interactions of the human form upon the earth cause disharmony, then the earth will find a way to restore its balance by any or all the aforementioned means.

However, unlike a human bio field, you cannot massage or direct energy in a sufficient quantity to ease the disharmony quickly enough to prevent the earth's response to it. There is a school of thought that suggests that if enough people send out healing energy to the earth, then it will respond and no major disasters will occur. Assuming that it is possible to do this, then we would firstly need to ascertain which of the earth's chakra points were affected, and, secondly, what form of energy was needed to bring about harmony in that chakra. But how can we direct enough energy from millions of souls into an area for long enough to bring back balance and harmony, let alone locate a chakra point that could be on the seabed thousands of feet below the surface? Nor do we know how many there are yet. Rest assured that there will be more than seven main ones. But I digress; let us go back to the human bio field chakra system.

Our human chakra system, which consists of the seven main ones, is not actually within the human bio field when it is born. It resides within the etheric light body, a system for self-repair that surrounds the nutrient matter that we call a body. It slowly moves into the bio field over a seven-year cycle (this is old knowledge; in some cases that timescale is way off the mark, as there can be an advanced or delayed crossover of each chakra into its final position within the bio field).

The generally accepted sites are the top of the head for the crown, the pineal gland for the third eye, inside the spine for the throat, heart, solar plexus, and sacral, and at the base of the spine for the root chakra or base chakra.

Now for a little more detail. For the first one and a half years of a child's life from conception, the energy core is grounded through the mother's connection. From around the age of nine months to a year old, the child makes its own connection, and its core signature is recognised and logged into the earth's Akashic record.

By this time, the base chakra has moved fully into position and the child starts to show signs of wanting to become less dependent on the mother. It has been recording since the first moment that the soul was delivered into the nutrient mass or foetus. But once it is connected to the earth and the universe through its energy core, things begin to speed up and new experiences are recorded at a phenomenal rate.

Should the bond between mother and child be broken before the chakra can get its own connection, by trauma or some other external dysfunction such as post-natal depression or the death of the mother, then damage can and does happen to the chakra itself, and its ability to record may become impaired.

It is also at this time that the possibility of a dark interruption of the child completing its core registry can occur, as the child's core starts to reach out to ground. If there is not sufficient protection from the mother, another core connection can be fused into the base chakra from a tainted energy source that is still on the prowl within all universes.

My team call this phenomenon a 'Chaos Link' as there will then ensue a battle of energies within the child. There is an old shaman analogy that the American Indians used for this: "There are two wolves inside of all of us, child." "Which one will survive?" asked the child. The shaman replied, "the one you feed."

If this happens then there is likely to be a delay in the subsequent transition of the remaining chakras, meaning that certain known conditions may materialise within the child. A lack of stability or indeed deep-seated fears of abandonment or rejection are often associated with this situation.

Similarly, if the sacral chakra is delayed it may result in an immature reaction to emotional situations (a temper tantrum, for example) that a 'normal' child within the correct chakra development cycle would cope with without a problem.

There can be a knock-on effect right up to the crown chakra transition, which will throw up many problems that should tell you that this condition is present (known as delayed chakra cycle syndrome).

There can also be the opposite problem of a child that has an advanced chakra development cycle. In this case it usually shows up as autism, autistic spectrum disorder or attention deficit hyperactivity disorder (ADHD) for the worst-case scenarios, and child prodigies in best-case scenarios. This is just a small sample of the related conditions.

Have you ever wondered why a child prodigy could walk, talk, count, and do many other things to a level way beyond the norm for their age group, or even play music when they have never been even taught to play at all? It is highly likely that they have a remarkably high spiritual vibration and have retained much of what was copied over into their Akashic records.

Their links to those records are strong, and they can and do access them for this enhanced knowledge or skillset. We must be careful with these children as they can suffer burn out at an early age due to the physical bio field becoming unbalanced with the spiritual connections.

When relating the same advanced chakra development cycle to a child with, for example, autism, it will usually show up after their break with the mother's grounding connection and the implementation of their own core connection. They become fixated on one thing at a time, or one of their senses becomes oversensitive to light, sound, vibrations, and so on.

It is almost as if they are filtering out all unrequired information except for the point of their focus. Usually this happens until they feel that they have exhausted the topic, then they may move on to a new focus. They too may have strong akashic connections, but it is as if the filters have been removed and too much information is coming forth. They cannot cope with this as an information overload causes them to want to shut down all areas of interaction. This, coupled with an advanced physical development well beyond their ability to separate their emotions within the reality of their surroundings, causes responses to some stimuli that are exaggerated out of all normal proportions.

The chakra system is connected to the etheric light body like a series of energy generators. As well as recording everything that happens to the human bio field, it supplies energy transfer to the etheric self-repair matrix by multiple connections.

The chakra acts like an inverter of energy, regulating the balance of positive and negative energy within it and passing through it. If, for example, it has fulfilled its primary energy function of supplying power to the etheric light body, then it diverts any excesses of each energy to other areas. If there is a lot of positive energy, it will pass this down the core into the earth and out of the front of the chakra, blending it with the surrounding energy. If there is an excess of negativity remaining after the bio field is balanced, then it too will be passed in the same way. But if there is already a glut of negative energy surrounding the person, it will be transmuted within the chakra and sent out as positive energy to try to restore the balance of the energies surrounding it.

So, to recap: the chakra system and individual chakras are recording devices for all things that affect the human bio field. It is also an energy generator with the ability to transmute any energy excesses.

That covers the seven main chakras in a little more detail. Now let us look at four more chakras in detail. We have one main chakra in each hand and foot. These are not recording devices in the same way as the seven main chakras; they are energy transmitters and multipliers.

Let us look at the feet first. These two 'minor' chakras are located underneath the bones in the arch of the foot. Their primary function is to send the energy that comes down the core into the core of the earth, and to receive energy from the earth and transmit it back into the human bio field, chakra system, and etheric light body.

They cannot transmute energy like the main chakras; they can only transmit and multiply it if required. Why, you might ask, would you need to multiply energy? If there is a weak universal core with very little conductive energy left after servicing the light body and chakra system, then what is left will need to be multiplied to become powerful enough to penetrate to the earth's core. Likewise, if the chakra is not fully clear and functioning correctly, it will not be able to draw up the earth energy and push it up the energy meridians to the heart chakra where it is needed. In short, what energy is drawn up is multiplied to boost its power to clear through any small blockages on its way to the heart chakra.

If either of these chakras become severely blocked with a build-up of stagnant or excess negative energy, then no energy will pass through and they will need to be unblocked. Sometimes these chakras can become damaged by trauma or redundant through amputation. If this happens then major energy dilemmas will occur if not treated quickly.

I will discuss ways to clear, repair or replace damaged or destroyed chakras later in the book. For now, though, know that nothing is unrepairable, as we have within us all the cosmic energies and building blocks to repair all damage that either has been done or will be done in the future.

Now let us look at the minor chakras in the hands. They sit again beneath the bones of the hand in the centre of the palms. They are the same as the feet and can process and multiply energy both ways. Have you ever felt that warm tingle travel up inside your arms when you sit in the sun with your palms facing up to the sun? These chakras are primarily for healing and the removal of excess energies or pain, by manipulation, massage, acupressure or simply rubbing on the spot.

When a healer (and remember, we are all healers) feels the need to draw down universal energy and direct it to an area of a human bio field imbalance, that energy is multiplied exponentially to restore balance, sometimes generating excessive heat. This is similar to the heat that is found in an electrical transformer, a known by-product of energy multiplication.

It is rare that these chakras get blocked as they are in constant use whether we know it or not. If an amputation of the hand takes place, then there is no entry or exit point for the energy to flow from or to. Think of a hose on full power thrashing around when nothing is supporting it.

Like an artery that has been severed, the affected energy meridians will close ceasing the flow of energy away from the remaining limb. How many times have you heard a person who is an amputee say, "it still feels like it's there"?

In the physical realm the hand or foot is missing, but no matter how long ago the incident took place, that itch remains. This is because another aspect of the etheric light body, the 'Etheric Blueprint', is constantly sending energy to a chakra that may not be there physically, but which is there etherically.

This interconnectivity between the universe, our energy core, our chakra system, our etheric light body and the earth's core, are all conducted via electrical energy impulses happening at a speed so fast that we have not yet found a way to measure it. We think that the speed of light is fast, but it travels at a snail's pace compared to the speed of these energies.

There are many other chakras within the human bio field linked to organs, tissues, and much more. There are also out-of-body chakras along our core both up and down. These are believed to relate to spiritual growth or may even be the gateways to other dimensions or universes. They are also transmitters and multipliers of energy, boosting our connections higher and deeper always balanced 'as above so below'. They all relate to our other dimensions or subtle bodies surrounding us.

As you can see from Figure 1, each of the seven main chakras are connected to an out-of-body chakra causing the formation of a subtle body. You can see the relationships between those above and below and one of the seven main chakras. Let us take one of these to explain it a little further.

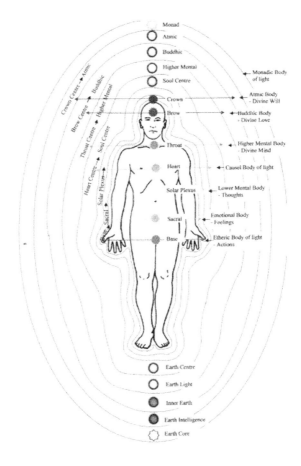

Figure 1

The soul, heart and earth centres are all linked within the causal body of light. The soul centre is believed to reside approximately six inches or so above your head. This is your universal information gateway to all the other fragments of your soul and connects you with the earth centre where your core signature is recognised. It forms the subtle body known as the causal light body. This is where you use your heart chakra to send out your energy to attract back to you that which you need to make you complete.

I say 'need' not 'want' as we do not always get what we want but will always receive what we need. How often have you heard someone say, "the answers are within you"? Well this is true, as you use your heart chakra to look within to find them. By looking within, you activate the gateway to your akashic records and can with practice bringing forth the answers to your own questions.

On a final note, regarding Figure 1, you will never reach a full monadic state while you have access to a human bio field host, for in the full state of monad there develops an ability to manipulate matter itself using vast amounts of universal energy to change one form of matter into something entirely different.

But this matter is still constructed from the same energy-based materials. It has happened before, but the human form could not cope with it, so it is now denied this ability to protect it.

There are also what we call 'shadow chakras' within the aura or biofield. These are energy recorders that store energy imprints from co-created energies from every interaction that we have in our lives. Unlike the internal chakras that record details or data, shadow chakras record and store energy from every interaction our human body is involved in. These stored energies can be both positive or negative depending on the interaction that created them, because for every action there is a reaction, and these energies are the reactive energy created.

Let us talk about how they can affect us in a few different ways. Take the 'laws of attraction'. Have you ever been involved in a situation where you were bullied by a parent or sibling prior to going to school? That energy remains in your biofield or aura. It should come as no surprise that some other people who have never connected with you before will take an instant dislike to you and begin the bullying process again. This is a case of like energy attracting itself to it; it is mostly beyond our ability to control the outcomes.

This may also explain why somewhere down the line, when the victim finds the strength to stop the cycle of events, he or she may go on to become a bully too. This is because they retain stored energy that was co-created during their bullying of both the bully and the victim, and whichever they feed will be the trait that rises to the surface at this time.

My team have also explained that this stored energy can be the cause of PTSD-related issues too. For example, if a soldier fighting on the front sees his best friend get blown up, there will obviously be an energy created that he would store because of the emotional connections between them. This will be a traumatic energy and immensely powerful.

This stored energy can then cause flashbacks and PTSD episodes where each time a trigger event happens, the energy is connected to the physical body and used to fuel that episode. I use the word 'fuel' deliberately here as this best explains what it is.

As we said earlier, every event carries an energy. So, if the already stored energy has caused an episode of PTSD, then more of the same energy is created. This energy can be and is used repeatedly, each time getting stronger than the last. It is no wonder then that many PTSD sufferers end up taking their own lives to end the destructive cycle of energy creation.

My team and I approach the delicate matter of PTSD treatment from a different angle than conventional psychiatric practitioners. We work on allowing the triggers to fade while we create a block on the stored energy's ability to fuel another episode. After all, when a fire rages uncontrollably, the easiest way of stopping it is to quickly remove any further access to fuel, thus allowing it to burn itself out.

Interdimensional healing

Very often a person presenting for healing may have been abused as a baby, and since they could not ask for help in a way that could be understood, another fragment of their soul would step forwards to give them energy for their protection. Should this happen, then immediately the second fragment's core connection fuses at the base chakras with that of the child it is seeking to assist.

I have seen both a human and an alien hybrid connection during these healings, and they were all fascinating for both me and the client. It seems that the alien hybrid was able to exist in both dimensions: our earth's dimension and to stay connected to its own planet wherever that may have been. I will cover this in more depth in another book.

CHAPTER THREE:
THE ETHERIC LIGHT BODY

If you refer to the chart in the previous chapter, you will notice that the etheric light body is superimposed upon the physical body. Not only is this the closest subtle body to our skin, but it is also fully interconnected and linked to the physical body too.

This is because when the soul fragment came down the mother's core connection into those early cluster of cells, it merged with them and, as they multiplied and grew into bones, organs, muscles and tissues, so the links grew within each new cell.

The etheric light body is our self-repair mechanism and holder of this incarnation's etheric blueprint. It is the carrier for the chakras before birth and after death of the human bio field host. It is also the fragment of our soul that we carry into this dimension with us.

To some gifted people this etheric light body is visible, much like the halo in old paintings of saints and angels or, to use a more modern comparison, the 'Ready Brek Glow' as seen in adverts for the popular breakfast cereal.

If you are fortunate enough to be able to see this subtle body, then you will have at your disposal a valuable diagnostic tool for the human bio field. By looking carefully at this light body, you can detect any thinning or breaks in its perimeter or distortions in its shape. This will directly correlate to an area of the human body and an associated chakra that is not functioning correctly.

As an energy healer I can connect with this etheric light body by passing my hands close to it. I can then transmit whatever energy is missing directly into this self-repair battery, or, if there are energies present that are in excess, then I can remove them and bring back balance. This form of healing carries many names, with reiki being perhaps the easiest to recognise.

There is another more direct and much more powerful connection that can be made by healers, one where we connect to their soul itself via a merging of both core connections. I will seek with my team to blend both my own core connection with the person's own core directly, creating one combined single expanded core.

During these healings I feel what the person feels as they feel it instantly. Through my team I can clear blocks, stagnant energy, damaged chakras and even influence the core itself. This is because the person's core will usually be weakened by blocks, damage, or the wrong balance of energies. I am the stronger element because I am in balance, allowing me to impose my will upon them for the purposes of healing their problems.

This is only possible because we all have the same etheric light bodies and energy systems. I like to think of myself as the jump leads needed to charge up the other person's battery with source energy. Once they are charged sufficiently, their self-repair system kicks in and uses the new energies provided. At the same time, their own core becomes more active, so the jump leads are no longer required.

I hope you are beginning to see that the soul is a complex sentient organism capable of self-repair given the energies required to do so. We are all unique in the DNA of our bodies, but we are all identical within the makeup of our souls and etheric light bodies unless damaged by outside influences.

This is what I mean when I say that we can all heal ourselves and others. We all have empathic ability if we just know how to interpret the signals required to switch it on. We can all open the mediumistic gift of spirit communications, because we are all the same spiritually.

CHAPTER FOUR:
TWIN FLAMES AND SOUL MATES

Following on from the soul discussions earlier, this chapter will explain how we see this delicate subject. It will also give you some ideas on 'soul families'.

As with all souls being divided this way was a way of weakening its ability to become too powerful, but neither was it allowed to become too weak. So, groups of souls came together in small numbers to create soul families or soul groups, and so they began to interconnect on a deeper plane of existence.

Within these family groups there would be multiple incarnations where roles were swapped regularly, including a mother becoming a child or a sibling becoming the parent. In these terms we believe that they can grow stronger spiritually through shared and retained energies from combined Akashic records.

'Twin flames' are generated by the multiple interactions of one soul fragment becoming the partner in many lives of another fragment from the larger soul group. There would be an instant attraction on a deep level, often resulting in a union then a breakup depending on whose energy dominates that union.

But most importantly, they are not from the same soul (occasionally you will get two fragments from one soul incarnating within the same generation in different places). Should they ever meet up there would also be an instant attraction, and possibly a union. But unlike the twin flame scenario, there would not be a dominant energy as they are both from the same soul. Therefore, they may be a male and female, but their energies would be perfectly balanced and harmonised.

There would exist an almost telepathic ability between them and an empathic link emotionally. This has nothing to do with physical attractions and everything to do with energy. Emotion, after all, is a strong energy.

I am fortunate because I have married my true soul mate. I am four years her senior and was born many miles from her but in the same country. We were both married in our early twenties to partners that were not meant to be our true loves, even if that is what we thought when we married them.

I was in my fortieth year when we first met and had been divorced for a year with custody of my three children. She had also been divorced for a year and had custody of her two children, so there were some remarkable similarities that brought us together.

But our children were not from the same soul families and there was discord laced with tolerance, which resulted in a lot of difficulties at first. But we provided a united front to all the children, and eventually some left the family unit. Others went to university and so the unit shrank until it left just us two.

It was then that my partner (we were not yet married) started to awaken and ask important questions. She went to see a spiritualist medium to seek answers and was told about her own ability in this field. She pursued her pathway diligently and, in so doing, began my own awakening process.

As we developed, we began to understand more. When we both walked the pathway of healers, we finally understood what a soul mate really was: the other half of us, the part that completes us allowing both to grow spiritually to fulfil our own potential.

We married after the children all agreed we should formalise our long relationship, twenty-five years to the day that we first met. That was five years ago this year (2021), so we have been together twice as long as either of us were married to our previous partners.

This should perfectly indicate the differences between twin flames and soul mates. On the one hand, twin flames will still struggle with energy differences regarding which is the stronger. On the other hand, there is equality in the soul mate energy as both are equal in every aspect.

FINAL THOUGHTS

This book has described what I call my new truths. Put simply, we are all unique physically, yet we are all the same spiritually. And what is our true soul's purpose in being here? To serve others before self.

If we all followed this simple truth – the same truth that countless messengers have relayed to mankind over the centuries – then we would end the need to dominate others, we would end the need for greed and the accumulation of all things in excess of what we need to live in the service of our fellow human.

This earth on which we live does not belong to any man or woman; it belongs to all men, women and children. When will we stop using the prospect of wealth creation in the teaching of our children? This early start to indoctrination is just the first step in continuing our descent down into a deep, dark hole.

This hole will become our own grave unless we radically change our whole approach to the teaching of our children and our children's children. There will always be conflict on the planet so long as those with the power take freely from those without.

We need builders to provide shelter, healers to help those who are ill, farmers to grow the food we need to survive. We need spiritual leadership to keep reminding us of these simple truths.

We need people who can transport farmers' goods to where they are needed most, engineers to construct the transport and the infrastructure to get it to where it is needed, and teachers to educate us differently.

But we do not need those whose greed shows that they serve only themselves. We do not need armies to fight against other armies for the right to steal what is on or under the land on which they are living. We do not need those people who set themselves up as more important than others, so that they can make laws to control those other people with impunity themselves. We do not need any organisation that places profit above sharing for all.

These are just some of my new truths, and if, like me, they resonate deeply with the very core of your being, then they are resonating within your soul too. Hopefully, like the healing of the sleeper cell, these new truths will radiate from your soul to every one of the five million-plus fragments, thus allowing change to begin and grow within all soul fragments that reside on this planet.

As always, I will leave you in Love, Light and Truth.

John Povey and my team of guides and inspirers.

APPENDICES: TRANSCRIPTS

During the process of compiling and writing this book, I have drawn heavily upon the many channelled writings given – sometimes as I sit and write at my laptop – by my team. The following transcripts should give you some sense of how these channelled writings work, what information my team wants to share, and even the visions that they have asked me to put into detail.

For me personally, the journey continues each day. I will continue to listen and learn from my team in the hope that what they share can be understood by many whose own journey is either beginning or has stalled in some way. I hope that you find on these pages whatever you need to proceed at your own pace.

There is no race to run on our individual journeys. We have within our hearts the desire to continue to place one foot in front of the other on our own pathways.

At this point I should explain a little about the transcripts that follow. Some are of visions that, perhaps surprisingly, I do not only get when in the state of deep sleep. Although I normally receive them when in bed trying to sleep, I can still hear my wife gently snoring and often our little dog, Jess, too. I can also hear the late-night traffic driving past our home, so I am not fully asleep nor awake.

For the most part these visions come through about 2.00am and may only last for 10-15 minutes while lying in bed. I am then urged to get up and write down all that I have seen, which is what I do. Strangely, this is when the finer details are put into my mind. This process can take a few hours but when I go back to bed, I ask that when I do get up in the morning the team wake me refreshed. They always do.

When you read these transcripts, I hope that you can see through my eyes to the higher meanings behind the words. In most, I appear to act as a saviour or hero, which reflects my great desire to help others. Our 'true soul's purpose' has featured heavily in my dreams since I was a child; always giving my life to save someone that I loved.

The other transcripts are of direct channellings that my team have brought through at various times over the past few years. These can happen at any time that the team feel is appropriate to enter my mind and write through me. As I said in the introduction, I left school with only the basics of education (my wife, an English teacher before her retirement, edits all of my posts on Facebook and even this book). Oddly, though, when my team write, there are no or very few corrections required. They obviously completed their education to a higher level than I did!

I often receive a snippet of information while in the shower; at first I wondered if the guides were in the bathroom with me! They have since explained why they do this in a way that makes perfect sense to me:

> "We are not there with you; we are out in the other dimensions. We are pure energy with multiple connections throughout all universes. We can connect to your core because we recognise your particular light and frequency or vibration. We send information down this core and, when you are in the shower, the water concentrates the signal inside the water flowing over you and amplifies it. Think of putting your head under water and listening to your own voice. You hear it within the structures of your body, your heartbeat is amplified, and any outside noise is muffled."

When you read these transcripts, I hope that you understand just how amazing my team are, especially when you consider that my writing ability is mostly self-taught unless the team step in (there is even one guide who writes poems through me!).

This picture shows how I feel the universal energy flowing down into my hands when we do our healing,

Seven-Year Chakra Cycle

Not only do we have a seven-year 'itch' in relationships, but we also have seven-year chakra cycles. The cycle begins at birth and starts from our root/base chakra and works its way up our body, reaching our 7th Crown Chakra at age 43. The cycle starts all over again at the root/base chakra and continues until our final day.

Each movement of the cycle gives us more depth to our life experience and personal growth. Each seven years is deeply influenced by the corresponding chakra. Aged 0-7 years, our root chakra comes into play, where the life force energy begins, and we do all that we can to survive. At the 7th year there will be a noticeable shift and change in behaviour as the next chakra phase begins.

At 7-14 years, the sacral chakra explores creativity, boundaries, and the discovery of sensuality as they start puberty.

The solar plexus chakra develops between the ages of 14 and 21, when we develop our personality, feelings, personal power and we feel that we have limitless possibilities and choices to make.

When we are between 21 and 28 years old, our heart chakra learns to love, feel compassion, and open our experience to friendships and relationships. It is a major learning curve because we are feeling emotions, but we cannot fully express them until our next cycle.

At 28-35 years, our throat chakra develops communication skills, and you can finally give a voice and express words more clearly by this age. At this stage we tend to outgrow certain friendships and relationships, as 'chaos' happens when we speak up and stand up for ourselves.

By the time we are 35-42 years old, we have new realisations, stronger intuitions, and sense of self. We can enjoy a deeper life experience and appreciation of our growth. When we reach the next cycle at 42-49 years old, we are drawn to spirituality, to seeking enlightenment, to finding some answers to the purpose of life. We seek unity. You may notice many in this age group wanting to get involved in community, religious or personal development activities.

What I find interesting is that the first cycle (0-7 years old) and the second time around cycle for 50-56 year old, would be going through the root/base chakra, and you may find that grandchildren and grandparents connect on deep level and share a good understanding.

If a traumatic incident occurs during the development of a chakra cycle, it may negatively impact the individual's actions and behaviour. They may show signs of re-occurring problems, or health issues in this chakra area. Healers and crystals can assist you during every phase of your cycle; they help heal past wounds and improve your overall wellbeing.

Can you just imagine for a moment how confusing your own chakra development must have been whilst you were growing up? Look back at your life to see if you can pinpoint your own age-related development as opposed to the seven-year cycle of chakra development that used to be the norm.

Now take that to another level, to that of a down's syndrome child, a child whose main function in life is to give unconditional love to all people without being asked. This, I am told, is because their heart chakra develops first instead of the base; they work in reverse from the heart chakra backwards to the base. Only when the base is complete can they work from there upwards to the crown chakra.

Similarly, an autistic child may fast-forward to the crown chakra in a really short time, causing them to receive energies and information so early that their minds cannot cope with it. This makes them close themselves off and set an intense focus on one thing only. This way, they zone out all the intense energies and thoughts; this for them becomes a different plane of existence.

27 June 2017, 3.10am

Background

Yesterday a good friend came up to visit me out of the blue. He brought with him a friend of his, Kam. I collected them from the station at just gone 11.00am. I returned them to the station at approximately 8.30pm that evening.

I will not divulge the mainstay of the day's events, suffice to say we enjoyed sharing of healings and the transfer of knowledge. But early in the day Kam said that she could do something for my hay fever which had become quite aggressive since waking that day. We stood in the garden and she started doing her treatment. My nose never stopped dripping from that point on. If anything, it got worse. We agreed it was probably a release of some kind.

After cooking some lunch and returning to the healing room, doing some more things and healings on Kam, we came back up to the house for tea and biscuits. While sitting at the table, Kam produced a small blue bag of crystal to see what I could pick up from them. When I placed my hand over them, I was immediately connected with what I thought was a guide of immense power, who proceeded to show and tell me things about the purpose of these innocuous little crystals. We did a small experiment with them and soon found more information and a stronger link; she gave me, at Dell's request, a small bag of these crystals.

My runny nose got worse. We went back down the healing room again to carry on where we left off. During this time in the healing room, I started to get an even faster runny nose and occasional violent sneeze.

When things had been concluded, we decided the time had come for me to return them to the station for their journey back home. I was guided to suck on a menthol sweet so that my nose was kept under some degree of control.

On the journey back home, having finished the sweet, the sneezing returned with a vengeance. It did not get any better once back home; I had prolonged fits of violent sneezing which exhausted me. So I went to bed, took two more antihistamines, and eventually dozed off to sleep at about 11.00pm.

Dream, or what felt like a video recording in my mind

I was first aware of an intensely vivid dream. But unlike those that I have had in the past, I was in a deep sleep, or I was not present at all in my body. Images of spheres of intense colour were placed within my mind. Ever so slowly, one by one, they were engulfed in a dark mass, almost like they were devoured.

There were three spheres remaining, floating there in a pale luminescent eerie light. From the side I could see this dark mass relentlessly march on towards these three bright spheres. Their colours were gold, pale blue and lime green. Slowly they drew closer together in a triangular formation and a circle of bright light began to grow from them outwards towards the invading darkness.

Then an equally bright beam of light began to flow from one to the other, growing brighter and almost white even though I knew the other colours were there. Its brightness was so strong that I could only see a bright white line of light going between them, forming a triangle with a different sphere at each point.

Then the green sphere moved outside of the circle towards the advancing dark mass. It was then that I noticed within the mass small pinpoints of vivid bright coloured lights which quickly faded away again.

The gold light and the pale blue light intensified, and the three lines of white light began to pulse almost like a heartbeat. As the dark mass touched the green sphere there was a blinding flash, and I awoke with probably the most violent sneeze I have ever had. It was so bad that I felt a very sharp pain in my heart as if I had had a heart attack. I looked at the clock by my bed; it was 2.45am. I blew my nose and got up to go to the toilet. I was told to put the bag of crystals under my pillow by a now familiar voice within my head.

After getting back into bed, closing my eyes and trying to get back to sleep, I received a massive download of celestial information, some of which I will write about now. At 3.00am I got up as instructed and got my laptop from where it had been placed in the utility room. I set it up on the dining room table and started to write the following.

The story of the big bang

Before there were planets, stars or any other solid matter that could be called a universe, there were many coloured spheres of energy freely moving around in what science calls 'space' or 'plasma'. These many spheres were content to just float and move erratically around, but one became mutated and started to get darker instead of brighter, almost growing off the dark plasma that they floated in.

As it grew it collided with some of these other spheres of energy. It absorbed them and grew larger in the process and more distorted in shape making it move slower, as if the plasma was resisting its ability to move freely.

This continued until only these three spheres were left. They formed an alliance where none had formed before, sharing their energy equally but the dark moved towards them relentlessly. I now understand that the spheres were sentient, alive with an energy that pulsed. They pulsed quickly, whereas the dark pulsed ever so slowly, almost imperceptibly slow as to deceive one into thinking that there was no pulse. When these three last bastions of free energy made their alliance, they knew that it was only a matter of time before the dark mass consumed them also. But when the green sphere went outside of the circle of light, it was not to attack but to sacrifice itself so that the other two could survive.

When the green connected sphere touched the dark mass, there was an explosion of intense magnitude. So powerful was the force generated that the dark mass fractured into millions of smaller particles, smaller spheres of dark mass surrounded by a very slight white glow. At the same time as this happened to the dark mass, the other two spheres within the circle of light began to connect with each dark sphere and increase the glow of light around them all. Not all the dark mass was turned into smaller spheres; some turned into a gaseous state and quickly moved away in a recoil-like motion from the light, as if to touch it would be its demise.

This was the big bang that science is trying to prove happened. It did happen. Those small spheres are now planets, suns, moons in many of what we call galaxies and universes. This was the start of a process of a coalition of energies that brought about a transformation creating the building blocks of the universe of energy.

All that we are and ever will be is in that energy. The two spheres that survived used their combined energy in conjunction with the remaining weaker dark gaseous energy, which is as we say unstable to bring about sentient life. We now understand this energy coalition to be the Yin and Yang, masculine/feminine energy, and when joined to the darker mass it gives substance. The dark element is the feeding energy that devours to survive and grow, while the other two are the balancers and restrictors to keep it in check. This is the energy that firstly created the universes and galaxies, then in turn created a living, cooperating energy matrix of all three in equal parts (the soul), tiny energy spheres, hundreds of millions of them out of a lot of the remaining gaseous matter.

Not all this dark gaseous matter could be harvested to create souls, and, for want of a better explanation, it hid out in the dark plasma behind larger planets and in their shadows to avoid being consumed in a coalition of energies. It therefore had to lose its ability to devour at will.

Unknown to the white male/female energy, the gaseous part the dark energy that originally mutated still retained this ability to mutate and found that by accepting the alliance of the three energies, they could grow stronger and mutate later. An infinitesimal part of this gaseous material still exists within all lifeforms as the mutant cell or sleeper cell, even as the remainder has become integral in sustaining all life forms, as part of the coalition of existence.

Now back to the crystals Kam gave me.

When that big explosion took place and that green energy sphere sacrificed itself, it contacted all the other spheres that had been devoured by the mutant dark mass. Every one of these new sentient spheres now created floating in the plasma has within it some of all those devoured spheres, as if they became a nucleus within each sphere like a connection point. They were sentient in a similar way as the 'souls' were, but in a different way.

They retained not only the green energy but a part of all of the devoured energies that worked to create a healing force of a constantly changing matrix of universal balancing energy present within each new sphere or planet that had been created. This energy would never die out. Even if its ability to exert planetary change expires, it will become like an inert material that conducts great power, a conductor of energy. When energised its power and influence transforms exponentially, but it does not have the self-generating ability anymore. It requires an external power source to be able to influence other structures with the same energy matrix.

In its current form as a crystalline structure, it is susceptible to external forces of pressure and would easily be crushed and become dust. But energised with enough power, it becomes extremely hard and pulses at a phenomenal rate, but only when powered constantly. Remove the power and it will quickly revert to the inert state that is has been found in today.

The images that were given to me regarding this material are that of a plasma TV screen. When powered up it will change to any picture sent through it. Turn off the power and it remains blank.

This is enough for today. It is 5.30am and I am going back to bed. I slept fitfully until I was awoken by a ring on the doorbell at 10.00am.

After breakfast and watering the garden and greenhouse, I was again asked to continue with the information stored within me. So here we go again, coffee to hand with my trusty laptop.

Plasma is a superconductor. Is it any wonder, therefore, that all space that we see is filled with this otherwise inert material? When you investigate space, it appears black in nature because it is in an inert state. But when energy is sent through it, the colours change. Therefore, some stars look as if they have a coloured tinge to them. Even the space that surrounds us as we sit or stand is of this same fluid material. But in the earth's case it is energised by Mother Earth itself. The objects that we see are created using this matrix of energies which are powered up by the earth. Electricity, often seen in films as a white energy, is in fact a specific element of energy travelling a speed through this plasma. Without an insulated conductive material (i.e. cable) it would just spread out and ground back to earth at the nearest structure that is solid and in contact with the ground. This energised plasma and the many and varied energy sources that are resident within it are the very things that we connect with to power up our etheric light body.

This is because our etheric light body is a fragment of the same material that the original souls were created from, as I have indicated earlier in this paper.

The process of the energy that created a soul, which is the same energy that created the planetary systems that we can see, is still going on today, as those two light energies move freely through the plasma seeking out gaseous materials to convert into new planets or stars as we call them.

Some of these smaller planets remain unstable as they may have a weak core of the other combined energies. Because of this, they become erratic in the way that they move, like a spinning top that is slowing down and wobbling all over the place. They then collide with or pull other planets into their orbit and spin faster gaining power. We call this a black hole, but, in fact, it is the dark mass reforming because it has lost the protection of the coexisting energies that were there at their creation, possibly having reverted to this energy type that devours all other energy forms.

That overriding source power moves through the plasma and, again, encounters the dark mass. Sometimes it causes another major explosion and creates more of the same planets, stars, moons, and so on. Sometimes it just diffuses the gaseous mass and breaks it up into smaller, less dangerous particles and they, in turn, race off around the universes (comets).

Some of the souls evolved rapidly after first being created to become sentient beings that had an overriding energy of cooperation and coexistence that which we call love, harmony, and peace.

These qualities were very powerful in the beginning of the matrix that is the universes. They would seek out lesser souls that may have sustained damage during their creation and, using their own energy, restore them to a full spectrum of all the required energies. This was the first healing to ever take place after the first coalition.

Slowly, as the aeons passed, these souls lost their powers to regenerate by taking energy into themselves freely. They started to become unbalanced as the levels of combined energy waned within them, and certain colour vibrational frequencies died. Those stronger parts of this energy matrix started to grow unbalanced again. These souls would roam throughout the plasma seeking planets, stars, and moons where there was still a strong presence of the initial building blocks of the universes, to take from them what was required to rebalance themselves.

Lemurians were one such species that the original souls created. But they were few always; theirs was a thankless task of travelling to repair energies that were out of balance, then returning home to regenerate their energies themselves as the planet they were drawn to had massive deposits of the energies that are the building blocks of all things. Some others of these original souls created would not allow themselves to become reharmonised and would move away so that they could not be touched directly.

They continued to grow stronger and darker and misshapen, and found that they could no longer travel freely through the universes at will. It all became too much of an effort, so they created a power-based dimension, one in which they could move freely about and could draw other souls towards it. If they were drawn in, they were consumed and became part of that mass.

This is the dark dimension that we call 'hell'. By separating itself into much smaller particles, the dark mass found itself once again able to move freely again in the plasma of the universes. It would send out energy to weaker souls that were moving around and drain them further, creating a new dependency between them. This can be reversed by rebalancing the energy matrix within the souls. Other souls have this ability as the energy combination you require is one of love, the original force of the sacrificial energies.

Enough for today. I am tiring from this new connection. John Povey.

2 July 2017 – Interdimensional overlap

I was asked to do some healing on a friend that I had not treated for over a year or so. While I was looking at something that had gone into her shoulder when she had an operation many years ago, I found a grey substance that was not negative energy. I proceeded with the removal using a pineapple quartz generator and was confronted by an image in my mind of a human/alien hybrid from another dimension. After my initial shock subsided, I asked what she was doing here in this dimension.

This was her reply:

> "I am one of her other selves from another dimension not in your world. When as a child she was abused and was too young to ask for help from her guardian angel, I stepped in to help protect her but was unaware that I would become trapped or fused at an etheric level. I have been with her ever since as she has been with me, sometimes in my world but mostly in hers."

I said that there is a belief in our world that if you ever come face-to-face with yourself from another time or dimension, a paradox will occur that will end both beings. She said:

"A paradox does occur, but it does not mean what you have said. The paradox is that we are fused at an etheric level, and neither of us can disengage from the other. As you will find out, even death as you call it does not create a split of the overlapping dimensional states. It takes someone trained in etheric healing to facilitate the separation of fused etheric bodies."

I then asked my guides why was it that I never saw any of this the last time that I did healing on her, and why they did not tell me about the condition before. This was their reply:

"What would have been the use of us telling you all about the other dimensional states and what has occurred here? You cannot begin to understand that which you just could not comprehend some six months ago."

I then understood their reply. How could I do any healing on a condition that I did not fully understand? How could I explain what I saw in my mind to my client if I could not comprehend what it all meant?

Now that they have both opened my eyes and expanded my knowledge, I am waiting to be shown how this anomaly can be rectified.

4 July 2017 – First removal of interdimensional being (deceased)

How clever are my guides? Today, out of the blue, another client with similar problems as yesterday's (sexual abuse as a child) rang in desperate need for a healing. I was told that she also had the same condition of dimensional overlap, but, in this case, the other self was in this world but had died some 12 years ago. This coincided with a stroke-like condition that my client suffered from but many a doctor could not diagnose as all the tests for a stroke came back negative.

I have treated her for an aneurism of the brain which has largely been successful. However, today, they have told me that she is my first practice client, in order to help yesterday's client. I spent a long time explaining what I now knew about her condition and that today we will separate both etheric bodies and the deceased one will just fade away.

Treatment summary

I was told to construct a special crystal grid to both anchor my client and be the division point at her feet. I was instructed to use the special Lemurian wand, and to visualise a white light laser emitting from its point. I started at her highest point of spiritual connection and worked my way down the body to the centre of the grid that I had set up there. I was then told to step to the side that the overlap was most prominent and again use the wand, but this time I was to visualise attaching it to the deceased other self and gently pull it until it was clear of my client's body. As I completed this, the other self faded and disappeared completely. I then used a sceptre rose quartz generator to infuse and fill any remaining voids with this energy to prevent anything else from getting in there.

I did some other chord cutting and energy realignment before finishing. When the client got off the healing couch, she said that she felt calmer and lighter and more energised. It remains to be seen what the long-term effects will be on this vulnerable lady.

22 July 2017 – Visions

I was awoken at approximately 1.30am. I had just returned from the bathroom to find that I could no longer sleep as a vision or altered state dimensional shift had taken over me. I could still hear the odd car passing by on the main road and was aware that it was raining heavily. Les was sound asleep next to me and the dog's breathing was steady upon the pillow behind my head.

The following is a description of what I saw.

It was a bright sunny morning and very warm. I was in my t-shirt and underpants as I got up to let our Westie, Jess, outside for her morning wee. She bolted down the garden path barking madly, which is unusual for her. Then the barking ceased and was replaced by a panic-stricken wail and then whimpering. So I ran down the garden path, semi naked. What I saw terrified me beyond words: the biggest python I had ever set eyes upon was in the throes of crushing its next meal, Jess. I rushed forward, screaming at it to get off. I grabbed its head, then a strange calm descended. My fear was replaced by anger and it was rising quickly. I communicated via telepathy with the snake, squeezing its throat with every ounce of strength that I possessed. I said to the snake, "do not turn me into something I do not wish to be." As I looked deep into its eyes mere inches from my face, there was a shift as it uncoiled from around the now panting but almost lifeless dog. Then I felt those coils envelop my body instead. I lost my footing as its coils tightened and fell to the lawn where I ended up on my back looking up into the sky.

I still had both hands around the throat of the snake as I looked directly at the sun and sent out my telepathic prayer: "I need your power now more than ever." And with that, I started to feel a temperature change. I began to get hotter and hotter. The snake tried to uncoil, but something would not let it. *I* would not let it uncoil. I was keeping it there with a power that I knew that I had but did not understand how I had manifested it. I was going to kill this snake; I was going to burn every fibre of its being. I was so enraged.

Then the smell of burnt flesh began to fill my nostrils. I did not know or care if it was the snake or myself, but I was wrapped in a charred skin, be it the snakes or my own, I was unsure.

By this time Les had come down the garden and was screaming. I spoke to her in her mind and told her to get the hose and wash the caked skin off me. She calmed at the sound of my voice and did as I had asked. Steam began to rise as the water hit me, meaning that Les could not see what was happening. After a while, the water cooled me sufficiently and the steam began to dissipate. I was still laying on my back on a scorched lawn, naked and totally changed. My skin was alabaster but with what looked like a sparkling sheen to it. I had two arms and legs and a torso, a head with pure white hair hanging down to my waist, but no genitalia.

Strangest of all, I was willowy and about 9 feet tall. An eerie silence surrounded us. What was I? Who was I?

We went indoors. I do not think that Les would have believed what she saw unless she had been there when it happened.

Change scene: I am now dressed with sheets draped over me. I am in a large hall healing all kinds of diseases for all kinds of people. They keep coming through the doors. I feel happy, serene and at peace. I am back to being what I really am: pure energy encased by a translucent skin, a Lemurian.

Change scene again: I have been tricked into addressing the United Nations, but instead I am imprisoned deep within the earth by the CIA. I tell them, "if you do not let me go within the hour, I will unleash the energy of the earth upon you. You need to evacuate this facility." No words passed my lips but every device capable of seeing the written word showed what I had said within my mind. I was communicating via their own satellites and computers.

The hour was halfway up when I asked how long it would take to evacuate the people here. The arrogant response was, "we are going nowhere till we find out what you are and where you came from."

I said that time for them was running out. My anger started to rise. Twenty minutes later I asked via the computers, "have you got everybody out yet?" The response came back: "why? We are so deep underground that nothing on this earth can get to us."

Another ten minutes passed. A voice came over the speaker system saying, "we said nothing could reach us down here and your hour has nearly passed." With that final comment I called upon Mother Earth to allow me to breach her mantle, to which she willingly complied.

I started to draw up the molten core of the earth towards me. The facility began to shudder, the panic set in and people were running everywhere. I said, "you arrogant fools, you have condemned your whole continent to destruction. The retaliation is not from above where you thought it would come from, but from below the earth itself." And as those final words echoed around the facility, the magma exploded upwards with such force that it blew the facility and the mountain range that it was buried under apart.

The ash clouds went high into the atmosphere, but as I emerged unscathed from the remains of the mountain, I brought up a shield that surrounded the whole of the United States. Nothing escaped that shield. No planes could fly over it and no ships could pass through it. Even though the whole continent was not yet affected, I turned to the sky and sent a message to the world via every satellite:

"I am taking back all of your weaponry. Look and all you will see is dust: the particles that you stole from this earth to create your own destruction. Your refineries, power stations fuelled by oil, gas, nuclear and fossil fuels no longer exist. They too are just piles of dust. Your boats, planes, and cars are all gone.

The only energy that you may retain is solar wind and wave based. Your greed and arrogance have set mankind back many hundreds of years. All the information relating to the things that I have removed will also be removed; not only in the written word, but all digital records will be erased as will the knowledge within the minds of your scientists."

I then drew up several more shields around other continents and said:

"Your ability to survive this will depend on each continent's ability to survive on what it can grow using its own resources. You cannot communicate or travel outside your own continent. You will now be monitored in ways that you never thought possible. Crimes will be punished, and corruption will be punished. Unless you all work as equals and share all that there is, then mankind's days are numbered."

9 April 2018 – Healing and meeting with Ancient Indian guide

Today I was honoured to communicate with an Ancient Indian guide. She said to just call her 'Mother'. She will soon become a valuable guide to a Star Seed healer that I have been doing clearing work upon.

This following is what I was told during our brief conversation:

> "I am from a race of peoples that precedes the oldest of your known civilisations, older than the Mayans, Egyptians and your oldest Asian cultures. But there is no way that you can prove this fact because we were a nomadic race. We had several places that we would frequently migrate to throughout what you call the Americas.
>
> We did not build temples, or any other structures that would still be standing now. Our lodges have long since gone back into this earth that we borrowed it from.
>
> The leaders of our tribes were the oldest and wisest of women, usually those with shamanic powers. We would never cut

our hair as this was our method of communicating our heritage. It would be as you see it now, braided into two long plaits with the feathers woven into them. Sometimes we would add shells and grasses too. The men were the hunter gatherers and defenders of the tribes, while the women raised the family and passed down folklore and spiritual wisdom from the Ancestors and great Spirits.

In time, the menfolk began to complain that they should be the leaders as they did the hardest work. The chief's head dress is still used as a symbol of authority, as is the ceremonial pipe of peace. These were the things that we women set out as teachers of the old ways; they even took from us the shaman's role.

We have long since moved farther out into the universes to continue to grow and learn, but, like now, we often choose one of our own to work with and send their soul's fragment back to this earth to do great works. The child that you are working with is one such fragment. You were quick to spot her potential and offer her the help that was needed to clear the way for myself and other guides to work with her. We thank you for your works so far and will continue to work with you during her initial tentative steps along her pathway.

You were somewhat surprised to find that as a star seed, she has over 100,000 dimensional fragments scattered throughout the seven universes, but very few earthbound lives that she could rely upon. That is why she was sent to you, to further her awakening into her purpose.

Your advice to her to remain humble shows us that we were correct in sending her to you. Your guides and especially your father, Little Elk, often sit with us, and we use your life stories to share the knowledge that each of you are learning at this time. Your world is changing so fast that we often cannot keep up. That is why we meet often, so we can learn from your experiences.

I have given you a picture in your mind of the location for you all to meditate upon to meet with us. Your drawing does not do it justice; a skill you have neglected for too long, child.

When we feel that she needs to expand her knowledge more, we will come through again in the place you call your sanctuary, a fine place to sit in the comfort of nature that surrounds your home. The measures that your guides have placed there through your work have pleased us all and make it a place we can visit easily when we feel we need to speak with you all.

Go in peace child and keep doing the work that has been set before you. There will be many more souls in need of the skills that are available through your connections to the great spirits."

Author's Note

This guide has requested that I write her story. When time constraints permit, I will continue to connect with her and continue writing that book too.

We will sit and write that story, and, in that process, we will learn more about not only human history, but also how those in spirit are now coming through to those like myself to seek a co-operative soul to spread their words, amongst those who wish to learn from them too but may not yet have a connection strong enough to do so directly.

26 June 2018 – PTSD research

I have for some years been guided to the understanding that most PTSD sufferers are being treated by the mental health sector, using psychiatric practitioners.

The view that I am proposing has a significantly different approach. I would suggest that PTSD in the modern military is started within the training process. I believe that the systematic breaking down of each recruit is a major factor in setting up the recruit for potentially becoming prone to future PTSD.

Yet, this is only a hypothesis based on my own military training, and my subsequent practices as an Energy Healer. I have been trying for several years to work with people who are diagnosed with PTSD, so that I can establish a database of information to support this hypothesis.

I have had limited success in convincing those affected that maybe a holistic approach would be a suitable addition or alternative to conventional therapy.

What I am guided to understand
PTSD is not in the mind; it is within a person's energy fields. It is the energetic frequencies of a particular event or series of events that are recorded within the chakra systems and auric fields of the subtle bodies associated with the chakras.

I have found that the person who suffers from PTSD has an enhanced empathic ability. In other words, when in a normal state, they are able to tune into other people's feelings and moods. They care about others before themselves (an admirable quality for the military), they feel that the role they are trained for has a purpose far beyond what the military requires of them, and they would do anything to protect their loved ones.

They often must put on a macho front to other military personnel to show that they are as strong mentally as the rest of their mates. They get embarrassed to talk about this ability to sense what others are feeling. They are particularly good listeners and usually sage givers of advice on many subjects (does this remind you of someone close who is suffering?).

I had the privilege to treat one such person a short while ago. He shall remain nameless as he is still undergoing treatment. When I saw and treated him, he was getting flash backs and struggling to cope while both holding down a job and advising others with a similar state of being.

I found that he was not connected either up or down to any universal or earth energy. When I asked my guides if this was to protect him, the answer was "yes" and that "his core was disconnected due to his ability to dimensionally slip." This causes the person to slip back to the event that troubles them. The event itself replays from the stored data within the chakras and energy field (flashbacks).

During the reconnection process he informed me that the flashbacks were starting again. I immediately stopped the process and was guided to a particular crystal to use at his Higher Mental chakra (approximately six inches above the head – this is the gateway chakra to other dimensional states).

His response was almost immediate. He said "the flashback stopped. What did you do? My therapist takes ages to subdue an attack like this." I told him that my guides had closed that gateway and he should not be able to dimensionally slip again. He began to feel much better and we discussed the types of treatment he had been given. At one point I said to him about the cords he had created and which were attached to him from others; energy links to the people who his trauma was centred around. He said in surprise that only his therapist had told him that before.

The outcome for him is a good one, I feel. The next time I see him, I will cut the cords. This will remove some of the potential triggers. I have given him a mantra to use daily, morning and night for at least 21 days to strengthen and stabilise his core. I gave him a visualisation technique to prevent him either cording others or them cording him, and I also treated some of his other physical health conditions.

During my journey home, during periods of stoppage due to traffic jams, my guides explained that the reason that not all people are affected by PTSD that witness the same events is the effect of the empathy ability.

Those who are empathetic are 100 times more likely to go on and develop full-blown PTSD than those who have zero empathy. If you are trained to kill any enemy of your country, then the best person to do that without asking questions is someone with no empathic abilities.

I look forward to meeting some other people who have PTSD so that I may further my research into treating holistically their condition. I feel that with most cases they will need no more than five treatments to clear it completely. This is what my guides tell me, so it is now a case of 'wait and see'.

To be continued.

15 September 2018 – Workshop with Helen Scott

During this workshop I was paired up with Paula. We were instructed to give energy via our hands to each other. First, the one with their hands-on top would give energy and the other person with hands below would receive the energy given. However, this did not work out that way with us. This is an account of what happened during this twenty-minute exercise.

As Paula's hands touched mine there was no transfer of energy. Instead, our respective energies melded together into something so powerful; I have never experienced anything like it. At first, we took a little time to find a balance point for this energy we were creating. Once we had lifted our hands upwards to about the heart chakra level, we found it.

Then all of a sudden our energies started to spin clockwise, getting faster and larger until it felt as if we were inside a tornado or vortex of energy completely surrounding us. Then, slowly, our connected hands raised as high as we could reach whilst sitting facing each other, and as this happened we both saw ourselves with our eyes closed deep in the universe. We came to a point where three spheres of energy came together in a triangle within a circle of white light. I asked Paula if she was seeing the same as I was, and she said yes. I then asked what colour the spheres were that she was seeing. We both saw an indigo blue and a yellow/gold, but the third one that we saw was different.

I saw it as a pale green, but Paula saw it as a bright white. Then, slowly but surely, it became the Yin Yang symbol incorporating both the green and white unlike the traditional black and white that we all know.

Then we agreed that on top of our hands the temperature was cold but below was warm. Instantly it seemed as if this vortex of energy turned upside down and the underneath of our hands and our bodies became colder. Our hands started to lower naturally but not under our control. They continued back down almost to rest upon our knees. We were then told it is time to change over, so, in response, our hands rose up to the balance point and I said that we needed to split our energies. The vortex began to shrink back into the space between us and then split in two and moved back within us.

We were both breathless with excitement over this thing that we had simultaneously experienced. But before I explain what happened when we reversed our hand positions, I need to say that it felt like we had been on a long journey through time, far longer than the ten minutes or so that had elapsed – it was as if many lifetimes had passed. I was given an explanation as follows.

We had joined our core energies to become one, and in the process multiplied their power exponentially. We had gone deep into the void in which all universes reside and seen the energies of creation.

We had then taken an enormous amount of this energy within the vortex and brought it down to the earth plane. We still felt the energy around us. It was tangible, electric and fascinating.

We then joined hands again and the instant we did the same thing happened. My hands were on top and Paula's below. This time we went down and as our hands physically could no longer go lower because our knees were stopping them, spiritually we kept going right into the core of the earth. We grew hotter and hotter until we had to leave. Our hands began to rise to the balance point around the heart chakra level, then the spinning stopped, our hands began to sway from side to side, and we both said that "this is now water that our hands are in." We were creating waves, and they got stronger until the power was that of a tsunami.

We were both told that healing the water is the way to heal the earth, as the water touches all the land masses. Then Paula said, "it does not stop there. As the water evaporates and becomes clouds that drop rain, very few places on the earth's surface are not affected. So by healing the oceans the water that falls as rain will heal the land."

It was time for this exercise to end. Separating was hard as neither of us wanted to lose this new connection. For a long time afterwards we both looked at each other and said, "are your hands tingling? Is there a spinning sensation within your head?" We were both beaming with smiles like naughty children who had found the biggest sweet tin ever.

I have met a lady who I did some healing on that sits in a group that sent healing energy into the seas. I will make the effort to connect with her again to see if we can all work together.

In closing I would like to thank Helen for bringing us together for this wonderful experience, and also Paula, my willing ally on the journey that we shared. Mainly I would like to thank the Universe for allowing us to be a part of it and for sharing its wonders with us.

Updated information regarding what a chakra and energy system look like

Firstly, we need to know that the crown chakra acts like a prism in that it can separate out the white light's individual colours. We have been told many times by many cultures that chakras are energy centres and that they are coloured red for the base, orange for the sacral, yellow for the solar plexus, green for the heart, blue for the throat and indigo for the third eye.

When I see a chakra, it is crystalline and shining like a star. The colouring as described above is how universal energy or white light is separated out through a prism. It was also described as imitating the rainbow colours because when sunlight shines through raindrops those raindrops act like a prism. The other thing of note is that the chakra is based on an eight-pointed star system, with a vertical line acting as the core connection that has around it a spiral vortex rotating clockwise as you look down on it from above, a horizontal line acting as the feeder of the relevant energy into the auric field, and both of the other diagonal lines acting as a positive and negative sweeper system. One will be a positively charged axis and rotate clockwise as you look at it. The second one will be negatively charged and spin anti clockwise.

This oppositional spinning around the axis point is similar in its effects as a gyroscope, keeping everything stable and functioning correctly so that the vortexes can draw down universal energy and draw up earth energy or reiki.

The most powerful of these chakras is the heart chakra as this is the meeting point of both energies. It has the greatest influence over the auric field's energy status and allows us to command its size and strength. All the chakras deliver energy to the auric field in the same way, and when you have an aura photograph done the resulting colours of the auric fields shown will show which chakra is dominant at that time. Often they are misread as they will be needing correction, but if they took another photograph ten minutes later, the colours will have changed.

Now if we look at these rotating positive and negative sweepers, we can see that they are constantly spinning to collect and transmute the energies they pick up. These energies are then transmitted outwards into the auric fields or down into Mother Earth, or if they are below the heart some may be transmitted there too. If the chakra is above the heart it will not draw up any energy, it will transmit it outwards and downwards only. This is indicative of the throat, third eye and crown chakras so that no tainted energy is permitted to contaminate the universal energy.

If either spinning collecting arm of this gyroscope gets damaged or contaminated by sticky energy (good or bad), it will begin to slow down and eventually stop altogether. This is when we feel out of balance because one side of the system is too heavy and it sets up a dissonance within the chakra, a wobble if you like until it stops completely. Then we begin to feel sluggish and drained of energy.

It is possible to repair a damaged chakra element by downloading through the healer's core the relevant particles from the stored chakra blueprint. It is also fairly easy to clear any blockages and restart the rotation of the chakras. The harder things are the replacements of chakras from severed limbs, because if someone loses their leg or arm then they also lose the associated minor chakras from the foot or palm. If through trauma or operations a chakra is damaged, sometimes it cannot self-repair. Think of multiple caesarean births, or of catastrophic injuries from explosions.

Not enough is being done to help those people who have had amputations where a chakra loss has occurred. One is bad enough, but if both are gone then the effects are cumulative and their recovery becomes harder. Without the correct energy flow it is just like a surgeon closing off the ends of arteries and veins and not joining them up: the circulation dies off, tissue damage and rot sets in, and eventually the person dies. But correct the circulatory problems and the remaining tissues will continue to survive and the person's life will be saved.

But we need to do the same things with the energy system too. By correcting the problems of a missing minor chakra, we can get the full energy system working again.

By grafting on a replacement foot chakra onto a stump of a leg, even if the person wears a prosthetic leg, the energy will flow down it into the ground, and that phantom itching sensation will disappear. We as energy healers need to embrace the abilities that we have and convince those affected by these traumas that we too should and could play a vital role in their healing process.

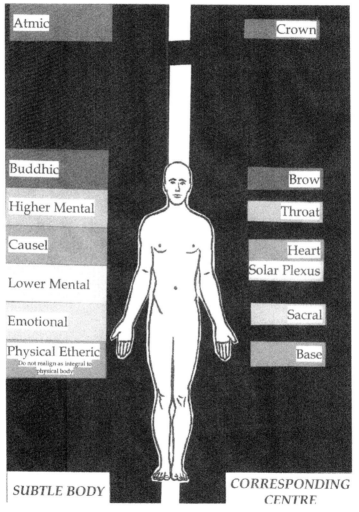

Figure 2

81

17 April 2019 – Healing at Outreach clinic in Suffolk

Today I have discovered some new interesting healing related facts whilst working with one of my clients who is also a student of my energy healing program.

She presented as having been getting extremely tired over a long period, and literally having one minor infection after another, probably lasting for a period of two to three months. Normally this lady has an incredibly good core connection and is well within the Atmic range, which was also balanced at her grounding point with Mother Earth. So, in essence, she was more than capable of healing herself and, as she is also a Reiki Master, other people too.

However, when I saw her yesterday there were some major problems with her core connection and grounding. Firstly, her connection point had slipped to the soul star just above the crown chakra, meaning that she was not grounded as no energy was flowing down through her to Mother Earth. In fact, the only energy that she was connected to was a contaminated reservoir of energy in a dimension that I have not been shown before.

The life spark connection was still there connected to through the soul star, but little or no universal energy flowed down her core. The connection point to this reservoir of contaminated energy was in fact the 'pineal gland'.

What I did see was a yellowish cloudy flow into the side of her head via the pineal gland. This, not the universe, was the energy that she was connected to. It had severed its connection as soon as the new one opened.

Before doing anything else, I had a long discussion with my team of guides for some way in which this lady could be helped. Like many of you, I assumed that the pineal gland was in fact our third eye, our higher spiritual connection or spiritual intuition point. But my team immediately corrected me by saying that the pineal gland is in fact another minor chakra point located between the crown and third eye chakras, and that it is like the hypothalamus, a master gland.

They described this pineal gland (which we all have within us) as a diverter valve (this is my team's way of describing things to me in construction terms that I can easily take on board). As such it is connected to a secondary source of energy, the contaminated reservoir, which is the same for everyone within humans. It only ever comes into play when the spiritual core has already reached out to the Atmic planes, and then, for one reason or another, the connection to the universal energy has been drawn lower down the core to reach the soul star. As soon as it goes below this connection point, the universe itself disconnects, so that the contaminated energy cannot flow back up the core of that person and contaminate the universal energy of source.

My guides described in detail how this gland does what it does. In short, it is reliant on the flow pressure keeping it closed. This valve has a small spring-like device, probably constructed of some sort of spiritual cartilage. When the pressure of the universal flow decreases to this dangerous point, the valve opens and connects to the contaminated energy. At that precise time your chakra system slows almost to a stop. The auric field collapses, almost as if the universe, chakra system and light body are putting you in isolation from your body. As the body craves energy of a spiritual or universal kind not available from food, it feeds off of the contaminated flow of new energy, thus making the body toxic and preventing any self-healing or, in fact, any type of healing whether remotely sent or hands on.

I have been discussing the prospect of this being another alien implant from our visitors many millions of years ago. They have indicated that this is so. Also, they have indicated that much of the information that we have regarding the purpose of the pineal gland is in fact misinformation to keep us in the dark about its true nature and to try to get emerging souls to connect with it in isolation as a shortcut to gaining spiritual insight.

So, we come to the topic of how we stop this from happening in other people. Initially my guides told me that to be able to stop the diverter valve from opening, you need to be working on it while it is open as I did yesterday. But obviously they have either researched it themselves or have contacted higher guides to solve the problem.

I have already created (under their guidance) a specific wand to do the job of closing the pineal gland's diverter ability down; not that I had any Idea at the time. So, for me to work on people with this wand to do that job from now on is purely a matter of incorporating the technique into all future healings. Simple, you may say. But what about all the people that I have worked with and who I have not found this problem with?

Well, my guides are still working on it, but they are telling me that it will be a mantra-based solution that is easily understood and simple to achieve with enough investment of the person's energy (think of it like the regular patches that you get from software providers to counter a possible virus). Simply setting the intention to do the job and repeating the simple phrases will deactivate this nasty little implant.

As and when more information becomes available or the mantra is given to me, I will write this up and publish it. I will print off copies and instructions for its use. It may take more than one healing to completely deactivate it.

29 April 2019 – Artificial joints, prosthetics and organ transplants

I am being guided to write this information regarding the pains that people feel when they have had a joint in the hip, knee or shoulder replaced.

The current thinking is that the new joint cannot be fitted until you have suffered a significant amount of degradation to the bones within the joint, whilst being prescribed stronger and stronger pain killers that have either addictive tendencies or serious side effects. It is also thought that further medication is required to combat the side effects, or you withdraw all pain medication and suffer excruciating pain.

Pain is how the physical body responds to a problem that is not in line with the etheric blueprint. Various electronic signals received within the brain activate enzymes produced by specific glands or organs, which are taken to the site of the injury to either surround the site with fluid drawn from within the body (swelling) or create more pain so that the person immobilises that limb or area (broken bones).

At this point I want to add something about artificial limbs and bone repair plates/rods. Some types of artificial limbs have connectivity built into the bone structures after amputations. I believe that a lot of military veterans are the main recipients of these; it is almost like a quick fit exchange system where different sorts of attachments can be easily changed.

I saw one of these myself in the 1970s on an SAS instructor who was instructing a rock-climbing session in Canada. His hand had been blown off in an explosion and he had an implant within and attached to the forearm bones. This allowed him to quickly change from a hook to a hammer or some other implement whilst being suspended on a rock face.

My own son and stepdaughter both have plates screwed into bones following severe breaks. Many people have rods fitted within the bones to support them during the bone regrowth during the self-repair process. So, to say that there are probably millions of people affected by this problem may well be an understatement.

Now for a little more in-depth analysis of this problem. If you have ever had a splinter in your hand you will know that the body sends white blood cells and chemicals to surround it. Along with this comes tenderness and pain and eventually those cells die off and changes to puss; this is all created by the human body. Untreated, it can lead to a blood poisoning problem. As the toxins build up around it and the pain spreads, the toxins start to take hold and begin to spread within the capillaries and possibly the veins. Then sepsis can take hold and poison major organs, and eventually they begin to shut down and die.

Now, the body has an etheric blueprint that shows exactly everything as it should be. When something is put into the body that is alien to that blueprint, then alarm bells ring and the blueprint goes into action.

If you take on board the fact that people are having organ and limb transplants, even though the doctors doing this work have perfected the replacement process from those dark days of animal hearts to the human-donated heart to multiple organs such as heart/lung transplants of today.

After the initial assessments of blood type/tissue type have been done so that the donor organ and the recipient are as compatible as possible, the exchange is completed. That person receiving the new organ would be given drugs to suppress their immune system so that it does not reject the organ. They may well have to be on that drug for the remainder of their life, and if they forget to take it as prescribed, their body will get infected because the blueprint is rejecting the organ seen as a foreign body.

So, if the human body can recognise a foreign body as small as a splinter to the replacement of a major organ that differs from its blueprint, then why is it that the medical profession does not give the same immune suppressants to hip, knee or shoulder joint replacement patients?

If I have now managed to explain this process in enough detail that you are beginning to comprehend exactly what is going on, then I will now explain how my guides have shown me how this can be resolved with energy healing. At the time of writing, I currently have one client acting as a guinea pig for this type of healing.

The person has had both hips replaced and is still in constant back pain. Even though they are a military veteran who has suffered a traumatic injury and a life-changing event, they have a remarkably high pain threshold, probably due in part to the original operations and nerve damage caused in certain areas.

During the healing when this information was passed to me, I was told that my team wanted to show me a way of surrounding the replacement joint in an energy shell. The purpose of this procedure was to use the person's own energy blended with universal energy to create the shell, which was then seen as it flowed over the implanted artificial components of the left hip only. Why only the left hip, you may ask. Well, this was the one causing most of the lower back pain, so my team determined that if we treated this joint, then during the next month we should see an improvement in the amount of lower back pain.

Simply put, the energy was used to confuse the blueprint into thinking that it was the original body part and not a foreign implant. By using this method of blending the person's own energy with that of the universal energy that supplies the etheric blueprint with its power supply, my team have informed me that the pain in the lower back will reduce, especially on the left side of the spinal column.

When we re-assess this healing to see how the client feels after one month – my team are not saying that one month will be time enough, only that this is the minimum time period to see if changes in pains occur – we will either repeat the process or, if there has been satisfactory progress, do the same for the other hip and any other implants that this person has.

For now, I will leave this subject open for any further information to be added either by other healers, or from my guides later, or after the client's next healing.

30 April 2019 – Update on pineal gland valve

Today my team came back to me with information on how this pineal diverter valve becomes activated.

This pineal gland valve opens through the original activation of the third eye chakra's cycle of maturation. To be more precise, in normal circumstances it would only activate sometime around a person's 42nd birthday when the third eye is programmed to open fully having reached its full functionality. Sometimes this may happen earlier or later depending on the individual spiritual entry point when incarnated into this life.

Here is the sequence of events. When the third eye opens fully, and the core connection rises to Buddhic and above and stays there, effectively you have removed the safety catch and activated the diverter valve's ability. If subsequently the person's connection point falls back to the crown chakra, due to either trauma or environmental activity of a densely negative nature, then the valve will divert to the dimension where this reservoir of murky, tainted energy is to be found: energy collected and stored and used by souls that have fallen from grace, not distinctly evil but knowingly using dark forces for their own selfish purposes to gain power over others.

My guides have told me of one such person that I have healed before prior to having this knowledge. The next time that I see this person, I will be able to see the tainted connection, whereas in the past I did not have this ability. Like all things in the universe, once you understand the knowledge the pieces of the puzzle fall into place. Then it is easy to recognise the same thing in others when they present themselves.

My guides are still researching how to create a mantra that will de-activate everyone's diverter valve. They assure me that they are close to perfecting it. It must be powerful, short, and easy to repeat daily. There will also be a time factor incorporated (the number of repetitions) done on a daily factor.

Information passed during removal of implant's activation ability on healing today

During the healing today, more information was passed regarding the levels of connection for this diverter valve. It seems that although I have seen the link to the tainted energy while healing the original client, who was used to act as a guinea pig to bring this to my attention, there is more to it than first thought as it goes in levels.

Let me explain. Our natural point of connection is with spiritual energy from deep within the universe or source. This reservoir of energy is the best available to all peoples, including extra-terrestrials, and all other life forms. What I now have seen in another dimension is this cloudy yellowish tainted energy, which the diverter valve can choose to connect the soul fragment with, but that is off to the left of the person laying on couch.

However, there is another dimension to the right that is even darker. In fact, it is pure negative dark energy that has been accumulating over aeons. This is where pure evil resides, and where soul fragments of evil people are stored in a dark duplicate of our Akashic records.

The souls that are trapped here are doomed to become either demons or walk-ins in varying degrees. During healings on people with a walk-in soul, I have retrieved their soul fragments and placed them within the etheric heart chakra, so when they eventually pass from this world they can go over to the light.

Because their other soul fragments are with them in the human form, the dark cannot take their soul fragments back as there are no links to that dimension now.

I now understand that the first tainted dimension is an intermediate level of energy that souls are connected to in order to use and become darker. Sometimes they ascend through this and cross over into the other side's reservoir to the right. Once connected to that energy they become so dark that when they pass, they are taken to that dimension instead of to the light or source.

I now understand that these are just two more of the dark's creations, alternate reservoirs of energy available to all souls. All it takes is for the implant to become activated and core diversion takes place.

It then is a case of how long you are using this tainted energy, and what you do whilst connected to it that decides if you can graduate to the next level of the dark energy. Again, should any more information become available, then I will pass it on.

Yours in love and light always, John.

This is the symbol that empaths need to visualise emblazoned upon a domed shield, covering the abdomen from just below the heart chakra to the base chakra, it will generate a force field around the empath that will prevent others from cording them, and it will also prevent the empath unconsciously cording the person they are helping.

19 August 2019 – Visions in the early hours

The first thing that kept coming through was a sense of foreboding, an impending event of great magnitude that has happened before and will do so again.

The message was crystal clear: "Stop the cycle of Greed." I was shown the area of planet earth that is bordered by the two tropics: Cancer and Capricorn. This is where I was told lies the greatest greed at this time, a circlet of it around the earth. There are extremely poor areas in this swathe of our planet with sporadic areas of obscene wealth, such as the gulf states, Singapore, and parts of the United States.

These are by no means the only areas of this planet that pay homage to the gods of greed. Many areas outside of the tropics have a far greater density of Greed Mongers per capita of the population. But within the tropics are the main sources of wealth creation: the gold mines, mineral deposits, hardwood forests, oil and gas, to mention but a few.

This is also where populations of people were traded as slaves for the Greed Mongers, wrenching them from homes and families, dragging them across the world and using these people to grow even more wealthy.

In the places where Greed is worshipped, these Greed Mongers have built multiple monoliths of a great height to show off their wealth in the form of super luxury apartments, hotels, and office blocks, sometimes combining all three within a single structure. There will also be towering slums to house the workforces that are trapped into working in these monoliths.

This was the background to which the visions were referring. The Incas, the Mayans, the Pharaohs and even some unknown Indian temples now lost in the Indian interior were all built for the same purposes: to demonstrate wealth and power over others. The Pharaohs even tried to take their wealth with them to the afterlife.

Each time that this world became so unbalanced by greed, a catastrophe of great magnitude has occurred to wipe out the imbalance and start over. Now whether these were brought about by extra-terrestrial interventions, meteorite impact, or an act of God, no one really knows.

But what science can tell us is that there were pole shifts, floods, ice ages and immense volcanic activity. This is where we are heading again. I do not know if it will occur in my lifetime or well after I am gone, but unless we start to change it is going to happen.

Global warming is a sign that the greed has risen to a dangerous level. Wars are and have always been fought and engineered by Greed Mongers, to either gain more land where great wealth lies beneath the soil, or to gather more slave labour to make it easier to gather these resources at a future date. This is what I was told will happen this time if things do not change:

> "The world as you know it will end with a dramatic pole shift whereby the main body of the United States will replace Antarctica, while China will become the North Pole".

This pole shift will cause the existing ice caps to melt very quickly, causing a great flooding as the waters rise too fast and too high for millions of people to survive in low lying areas. Because the flooding will cover a great deal of land, the water will reflect sunlight and the earth's temperature will fall rapidly freezing from the poles towards the new equatorial regions. Due to the rapid cooling of the earth's crust, pressure will build from within, causing tectonic plate shifts, upheavals of the earth's crust, and a resurgence of volcanic activity bringing previously undersea lands back up to the surface. It will take several generations for these salt-based areas to desalinate naturally and grow vegetation, which will, in turn, start a regenerative cycle slowly forcing the clearing of the ice back towards the poles:

> "Even though your planet has advanced technology circulating around it in space, you will have lost most if not all of your ability to communicate with it from the surface of the planet. Your specially built

and stocked bunkers that you have created will not save your race, as the period spent confined will cause several changes to the current physiology, and you will not be able to survive on the surface if the time comes that your bunker entrances are exposed for any survivors on the surface to open them."

"Your delusions that those with wealth created from Greed will have a better chance of survival are misplaced. No amount of money can protect you from what you are creating upon this planet. A wise man once said that the human race could not survive without this planet, but the planet would thrive without the human race."

"This message is being sent out by those of us in the universe who would help your race understand what it is doing to itself. Some of us have lived through similar things or our own history has shown us what not to do. But only those who seek the truth above wealth are able to interpret our messages. If the masses of your world unite to fight the seemingly few powerful elites, there is a chance to avoid the coming catastrophe. If not, then most of the air-breathing organisms and life forces on this planet's surface will destroy each other's possibility for survival."

"We leave you with this message in the hope that by sharing it many others will see the truth within. It may strike a chord within other cultures whose own messengers are foretelling similar premonitions that have been given to them."

"Take great heed of our words. We are forbidden to intercede within your race's problems, even though many times rogue elements of our own peoples have interfered in the past and could be said to be the original creators of GREED, as it was through their own greed that the concept was brought to your planet. For these insurgencies we can now only say we are extremely penitent for them, and we will continue to send messages of support from afar."

"One last thing we would like to pass onto you through this vessel. There are many on your planet purporting to be in connection with Star ships that will come to your rescue or specific enlightened beings that will step forward to save your race. These are false idols. The universal laws of 'what you sow, so shall you reap' are there to stop us from interfering within your race's decisions."

"There is but one exception to this rule and that is this: 'if you turn your attentions to other planets, without changing your reliance on greed to create a structure of society like that which you now live by, we will repel those attentions in the strongest manner possible'. We have learned our lessons as you should learn yours. Before you try to impose your race's values upon other planets, sort out a suitable alternative to GREED."

28 September 2019 – Additional information given

Today I saw another lady that I had done this type of healing on since that first client. She too was complaining of discomfort in the pelvic girdle area.

My guides told me that the pain that she was feeling was because with both hips replaced with titanium joints, the whole area was now like a radar dish (pelvic girdle). The energy that they placed around that whole area was akin to the paint that is applied to stealth fighters to disrupt radar images, as it flows over the entire area and the radio waves are disrupted and therefore cannot build up a resonance within the pelvic girdle. This resonance is what the human body detects and sends signals to the brain as pain.

We are, I am told, going to find many more instances of this as 5G takes hold, as these radio waves are extremely dense in their patterning.

Human bones do not amplify this resonance because of the porous nature of their structure. All those microbore holes running through naturally disrupt the signal, whereas the titanium, being high-grade metal, amplifies the signal as well as reacts with tiny vibrations (resonance). So, each time my team come across someone like this, they inform me of a way to overcome the problem.

If you live near enough and would like to take part in this case profiling, please contact me at Reaching Out Therapy (reachingouttherapy.co.uk) and we can see if you are a suitable candidate for adding to these case files.

In love and light always, John.

INDEX

Printed in Great Britain
by Amazon

59488396R00068